Destination Detectives

Germany

North America

Europe

Asia

GERMANY

Africa

South America

Australasia

Sonja Schanz and Gerry Donaldson

www.raintreepublishers.co.uk
Visit our website to find out more information about **Raintree** books.

To order:
☎ Phone 44 (0) 1865 888112
📄 Send a fax to 44 (0) 1865 314091
💻 Visit the Raintree Bookshop at **www.raintreepublishers.co.uk** to browse our catalogue and order online.

Produced for Raintree by
White-Thomson Publishing Ltd,
Bridgewater Business Centre,
210 High Street, Lewes, BN7 2NH

First published in Great Britain by Raintree,
Halley Court, Jordan Hill, Oxford OX2 8EJ,
Part of Harcourt Education.
Raintree is a registered trademark of
Harcourt Education Ltd.

Editorial: Sonya Newland, Melanie Waldron,
and Lucy Beevor
Design: Gary Frost
Picture Research: Amy Sparks
Production: Chloe Bloom

Originated by Modern Age
Printed and bound in Hong Kong

Hardback:
10 digit ISBN 1406203130
13 digit ISBN 9781406203134
10 9 8 7 6 5 4 3 2 1
11 10 09 08 07 06

Paperback:
10 digit ISBN 1406203246
13 digit ISBN 9781406203240
10 9 8 7 6 5 4 3 2 1
12 11 10 09 08 07

British Library Cataloguing in Publication Data
Schanz, Sonja
  Germany. - (Destination detectives)
  1.Germany - Geography - Juvenile literature 2.Germany -
  Social life and customs - 21st century - Juvenile
  literature 3.Germany - Civilization - Juvenile literature
  I.Title
  943'.0882

Acknowledgements
Corbis pp. 6b (Régis Bossu/Sygma), 18 (Richard Klune),
20 (Dave G. Houser/Post-Houserstock), 21 (Adam Woolfitt),
31 (Inge Yspeert), 34-35 (Michaela Rehle/Reuters), 36 (Régis
Bossu/Sygma); Getty Images pp. 5b (Sean Gallup), 26 (Sean
Gallup), 37 (Kati Jurischka/Bongarts); Photolibrary pp. 4
(The Travel Library Limited), 5 (Japack Photo Library),
5t (Workbook, Inc.), 5m (Robin Smith), 6t (Panstock Llc
Catalogue), 8-9 (Photononstop), 9 (Mauritius Die
Bildagentur Gmbh), 10-11 (Jon Arnold Images), 12-13
(Ifa-Bilderteam Gmbh), 13 (Photolibrary.Com), 14
(Photolibrary.Com), 17 (Jon Arnold Images), 19 (Robin
Smith), 22 (Mauritius Die Bildagentur Gmbh), 23 (Robert
Harding Picture Library Ltd), 24-25 (Jon Arnold Images),
25 (Plainpicture), 27 (Index Stock Imagery), 28 (Jon Arnold
Images), 29 (Robin Smith), 30 (Monsoonimages), 32
(Mauritius Die Bildagentur Gmbh), 32-33 (Index Stock
Imagery), 33 (Jon Arnold Images), 38 (Index Stock Imagery),
41t (Monsoonimages), 42 (The Travel Library Limited),
43 (Ifa-Bilderteam Gmbh); TopFoto pp. 11 (Michael
Rhodes), 12, 15, 16 (Peter Kingsford), 34 (Keystone),
39 (Ray Roberts), 40 (Keystone), 41b (Harold Chapman).

Cover photograph of German houses reproduced with
permission of Photolibrary/Photononstop.

Every effort has been made to contact copyright
holders of any material reproduced in this book.
Any omissions will be rectified in subsequent
printings if notice is given to the publishers.

The paper used to print this book comes from
sustainable resources.

Contents

Any words appearing in the text in bold, **like this**, are explained in the glossary. You can also look out for them in the Word Bank box at the bottom of each page.

Where in the world?

You awake to the sounds of bells. You check your watch. Although it is exactly 8 a.m., the bells don't sound like a church clock striking the hour. Instead, they are playing a sweet tune.

From your window you can see a crowd of people gathered in a square below you. They are all looking up at the tall building where the sound of bells is coming from.

As you watch, windows open at the top of the tower. Mechanical figures of knights on horseback appear, then soldiers with swords, and other characters. Finally, the smiling figure of a man appears. He drinks from a giant glass – and the windows close.

Festivals

Festivals are a way of life in Germany and take place throughout the year. Smaller towns like Rothenburg often recreate scenes from their history. There are other famous festivals in the larger cities, including the Oktoberfest, which is held in Munich in the autumn.

Tourists from many countries travel to the famous Christmas markets in cities such as Frankfurt.

WORD BANK bugle brass instrument like a trumpet but without keys
medieval relating to the **Middle Ages**

A medieval town

You wander into the square to find out more. Although it is quite early, many people are already shopping at the market stalls. Looking around you, it seems that the buildings in this town have not changed in about 500 years! Before you have a chance to ask anyone about the clock, you hear the sudden sound of drums, **bugles**, and men marching.

A troop of soldiers dressed just like the figures on the clock appears in the square, and lines up in front of the church tower. Looking up, you notice a banner on the tower that reads "Festival Rothenburg". So that's where you are – the **medieval** city of Rothenburg in Germany! You are here for the start of the town's great annual festival.

The town of Rothenburg was founded in 1195. Its name means "red castle", because a castle of red brick was built here.

Find out later...

Where will you find this fairy-tale castle?

Why is cycling so popular in Germany?

Which building is nicknamed the "washing machine"?

Germany at a glance

SIZE: 357,000 square kilometres (138,000 square miles)

CAPITAL: Berlin

POPULATION: 82.4 million

TYPE OF GOVERNMENT: Federal republic

OFFICIAL LANGUAGE: German

CURRENCY: Euro €

Your first stop is the tourist office to find a map of Germany. Looking at the map, you discover that Rothenburg lies right in the middle of the country. You can see that there are many different landscapes and features in the different regions of Germany.

The Black Forest is an area of gently rolling hills and woodland, ideal for hiking and cycling.

Germany's main **export** is motor cars and Stuttgart is the home of Mercedes Benz and Porsche.

WORD BANK   export selling goods to other countries
federal republic group of states under a central government

Hamburg is one of the most important **ports** in Europe.

The Baltic Sea area is a tourist paradise, with its spectacular coastline and island scenery.

Berlin is the capital of Germany and its largest city. It is home to the German Government as well as many museums, concert halls, and other cultural attractions.

The four quarters of Germany

Germans will often talk about the "four quarters" of their country. The River Main, which flows just to the north of Rothenburg, divides the country between north and south. Germany used to be divided into East and West, and this old border, together with the River Main, divides the country into quarters.

Bavaria is the largest of Germany's sixteen **states**. Munich is its capital.

The Alps and lakes offer some of the most stunning scenery in Germany.

port place where ships load or unload cargo
states areas of Germany that have a level of self-government

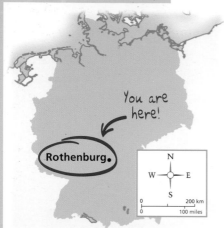

You are here!

Rothenburg.

N
W   E
S

0   200 km
0   100 miles

Germany's climate

Although Germany is closer to the Arctic than the **Equator**, it has a moderate **climate**. This means that generally there are no very long periods of either cold or hot weather. Warm winds can blow in from the North Sea, so areas along the coast have warm summers and mild winters. Inland, though, the climate is continental – there are bigger variations in the temperature. Winters are colder and summers are hotter.

Before moving on, you decide to explore the area around Rothenburg. It is a perfect day for a walk in the hills – a popular pastime for many Germans. You decide to visit the valley of the Tauber, the river on which Rothenburg stands. All around you is a landscape of rolling wooded hills and mountains, dotted with meadows. Many different crops are growing in the fields.

The German landscape

This is what large parts of central Germany look like, although the mountains vary greatly in height. Some of the mountains in the Central Uplands are over 1,000 metres (3,000 feet) high. In winter, the higher peaks are covered in snow, and people come from all over Germany – and other counties – to enjoy the skiing here.

People use skis to travel across the deep snow in Bavaria, in southern Germany.

WORD BANK   climate typical weather conditions in a region
Equator imaginary line round the middle of Earth

You really have to be in this part of Germany to be able to downhill ski. Your map shows you why – there are hardly any mountains in the northern part of Germany. Apart from the region of the Harz Mountains, low-lying **plains** stretch all the way from the border with Denmark, southwards as far as Cologne, Hanover, and Leipzig. In these regions, people use skis to travel cross-country. This area is ideal for a different kind of activity – cycling. This is another popular pastime in Germany, and there are cycle lanes in many parts of the country.

▲

Beach baskets (*Strandkörbe*) offer holidaymakers protection from the sun and wind on Germany's beaches.

Two coastlines

Germany has two stretches of coastline – along the North Sea and the Baltic Sea. The North Sea coast and the Frisian Islands are very low-lying and floods often occur. Much of Germany's farming takes place here and some farmhouses are built on mounds to protect them.

The Romantic Road

The Romantic Road was a trade route during the **Middle Ages**. It is 360 kilometres (200 miles) long and runs from Würzburg to Füssen. The road connects walled towns and villages, and almost all of them have a castle. The road got its name from the beautiful scenery along its route.

The Romantic Road starts in Würzburg, and travels through some of Germany's most picturesque countryside.
➤

Views of Germany

You decide to move on and see more of the German landscape. Rothenburg lies almost at the top of the "Romantic Road". The Alps and the fairy-tale castle of Neuschwanstein are at the southern end. You decide to follow this road to the south of Germany.

The journey takes all day by bus, but the road runs through some of the most beautiful scenery in the country. The gently rolling countryside of Upper Bavaria is dotted along the way with small **medieval** walled towns. Soon after crossing the River Danube, you reach the former Roman settlement of Augsburg.

The amazing Alps

Not far beyond Augsburg, the view changes again. The landscape is almost completely flat. By the side of the road there is always a cycle path. This part of Germany is known as the Alpine Foreland, and is ideal for cycling.

Looking ahead, you can see the dramatic view of the snow-capped Alps drawing closer. Your journey ends in Füssen. This is really the bottom of Germany, and the mountains of the Alps tower over this region.

The Zugspitze, in the southern German Alps, is the highest mountain in the country, at 2,962 metres (9,718 feet).

Germany's castles

Almost every region of Germany is littered with beautiful castles, many of them built in medieval times. Some are now ruins, but many are still standing. They can be very grand, often built on hilltops or mountainsides. Many have wonderful views of the countryside.

A bit of history

King Ludwig II

Ludwig II became king of Bavaria in 1864, when he was just eighteen. He was an unusual king, because he was more interested in music and architecture than in politics and government. In 1886, Ludwig mysteriously drowned. No one knows whether or not he was murdered.

Just before he died, Ludwig II of Bavaria was declared insane by the German Government.

As you explore the castle of Neuschwanstein, near Füssen, you wonder who could have lived here. In fact, the answer is – nobody. King Ludwig II ordered that a wonderful castle should be built for him, but he died in 1886 before it was finished.

The German Empire

The area that is now Germany was once made up of lots of smaller regions called **states**. Each of these had its own ruler – a prince, a duke, or a king. Ludwig was king of Bavaria. The area known as Prussia was ruled by King Wilhelm. In 1871, all the different states were joined together to make the German Empire.

WORD BANK chancellor chief minister to a king or emperor

Wilhelm became emperor of this new country. Ludwig II of Bavaria was allowed to keep his title of king, but he lost his power. Berlin was made the capital city of this new German Empire. The empire lasted until the end of World War I in 1918.

Ludwig's castle has been a good starting point for finding out about Germany's history, but to discover more, you decide to head to Munich. Today, Munich is a lively city, known for its famous beer festival, but it was here that the darkest period of German history began.

The castle at Neuschwanstein was the model for Sleeping Beauty's castle at Disneyland in the United States.

Bismarck was nicknamed the "Iron Chancellor" because he was so powerful.

Otto von Bismarck — the Iron Chancellor

Otto von Bismarck is one of the greatest figures in German history. He was prime minister of Prussia during Wilhelm's reign and it was his idea to **unite** the states into one nation. As the first **Chancellor** of Germany, he led the country to a position of great power.

You are here!

Munich •

World War II

When you arrive in Munich you begin to find out about Germany's history under Adolf Hitler. Hitler first gained public support in the 1930s by speaking to the crowded beer-halls in Munich. Life had been difficult for the German people since the end of World War I in 1918. The country had paid billions of pounds as **compensation** to other countries and many people were unemployed. There was widespread poverty and the people were very unhappy.

Hitler, who was leader of a political party called the National Socialist (Nazi) Party, promised to solve these problems. He said he could rebuild Germany, making it stronger and better than before. The German people believed him, and Hitler grew very powerful. In 1939, he led his country into World War II. During the war, thousands of people – including German Jews and gypsies – were killed on Hitler's orders. He was defeated in 1945.

Runaway inflation

In the early 1920s, Germany suffered from terrible **inflation**. The price of everyday items such as food and clothing rose very quickly. People needed a great deal of money to buy even basic things. Because of this, banks were issuing banknotes which were almost worthless. It was a very difficult time for the German people.

Adolf Hitler at a rally in 1934, gathering support from the German people.

WORD BANK   capitalist society where people can own businesses and resources
                 communist classless society in which resources belong to the community

East and West

After World War II, Germany was divided into two parts – East and West. The two countries were ruled by different people and had different political systems. When people from the East continued to move to the richer West, the East Germans built a wall to divide the city of Berlin in two. This made movement between the two parts almost impossible. Many tried to escape over the wall. Armed guards patrolled the length of the wall, and most people were stopped before they could reach the other side. Only a lucky few managed to escape to a better life in the West. The wall started being torn down in 1989, and the following year, Germany was officially reunited as one country.

In 1989, the wall that had been built to separate the two parts of Berlin was broken down, and people could move again from East to West.

Two Germanys

Following Germany's defeat in World War II, the countries Germany had fought against could not decide how to rule Germany. They decided to divide it up. West Germany was supported by the **capitalist** countries of the west, and East Germany by the **communist** Soviet Union.

compensation payment to make up for someone else's loss
inflation rise in how much things cost

It's time to leave Munich. Standing at the platform of the main station is the gleaming white Inter City Express (ICE), which will speed you to Cologne in four and a half hours. These modern trains connect all Germany's major cities, and are very comfortable. Other trains travel to the smaller towns and villages across Germany.

Autobahns

The German autobahns (motorways) were begun in the 1930s, as a way of moving soldiers and military equipment across the country quickly. Germany has over 11,000 kilometres (7,000 miles) of motorways.

Traffic on the Rhine

Halfway into your journey, the train arrives at the River Rhine and for the rest of the trip the train follows the course of the river closely. What fascinates you most, though, is the amount of traffic on the river. Enormous **barges** can be seen every minute. Some are filled with coal, others are carrying lots of containers to and from **ports** within Germany and to other parts of Europe.

An ICE train pulls into the main station at Cologne. These trains can travel at speeds of up to 250 km (155 miles) per hour.

River transport

Germany's main ports include Berlin, Stuttgart, Cologne, and Dresden, but this is hard to believe when you look at a map – some of them are hundreds of kilometres from the sea!

Barges or lorries?

Why do the Germans use barges for transporting goods? While a single lorry can deliver around 40 tonnes (39 tons) of goods along the 1,000-kilometre (600-mile) length of the Rhine in a day and a half, a modern barge can deliver 50 times that amount in a journey that takes two or three days.

Barges, like this one on the river by Cologne, are much better for the environment than most other ways of transporting goods to and from cities.

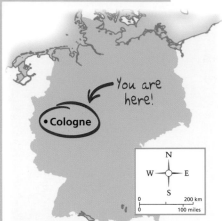

You are here!

• Cologne

N
W — E
S

0   200 km
0   100 miles

City transport

Soon, the famous twin spires of Cologne cathedral come into view, and your train crosses the Rhine and pulls into the city's main station. In Cologne, you soon realize that it is very easy to get around the city. Buses and **trams** run very frequently and the big "U" sign that you see every few blocks means that there is an underground train station there.

You are also pleased to discover that if you buy a single ticket for a trip across town, you can use it on the bus, tram, and train. Timetables are carefully planned so that you never have a long wait to reach your destination. What's more, you can even continue your journey on a bicycle free of charge! All around the city, German Rail has cycle stores. You can simply pick one up and then drop it off at the end of your journey.

Sharing the journey cost

It is becoming increasingly popular to share car journeys in Germany, when travelling from one city to another. Agencies register and bring together people making the same journey on the same day. This means that it costs less for the driver, and reduces the number of cars on the road.

Trams are common in Germany's cities, and are a useful and environmentally friendly way of getting around.

➤

WORD BANK   tram train that runs on rails through city streets

By bike or on foot

Cycling in the cities is perfectly safe, as there are special lanes for cyclists. To reduce air pollution in the cities, the German Government encourages people to use public transport or to cycle, instead of driving cars.

Of course, the easiest way of all to get around in the towns and cities is on foot. Most city centres are completely or partly free of traffic, making them people-friendly rather than car-friendly.

A cyclist's city

Münster is a cyclist's paradise. The centre of the city was destroyed in World War II, and when it was rebuilt cyclists were given special consideration. Cyclists have their own ring road, traffic lights, and parking areas. Around 43 percent of journeys within the city are by bicycle.

In cities like Frankfurt, cycle lanes run next to the traffic lanes on the roads.

Sausages

The choice of sausages in Germany is amazing! Many of them are specialities of a particular region, and the Germans take great pride in the quality of their sausages. Some of them are huge – they can be a whole metre in length!

Strolling around Cologne makes you hungry. There are plenty of restaurants, cafés, and bars here, with a huge variety of German and international food. You decide to try some traditional German food, and choose one of the many types of sausages sold at various kiosks. These are usually served with mustard and a bread roll.

Bread and meat

Afterwards you go into a bakery and buy one of the delicious-looking cakes. Bakeries like these usually have an enormous selection of different breads and bread rolls on display. They range from white to almost black bread, with or without seeds, grains, and nuts. Cakes and pastries are also very popular, and you can buy all kinds here.

Sausages are a favourite food in Germany, and most butcher's shops will offer a wide selection.

WORD BANK   barley grain used in making beer

There are also many different types of meat available in Germany. You have already tried one type of sausage, but there are hundreds of others, as well as several types of cold meats and some very odd-looking specialities such as pigs' feet and tripe (cow's stomach)!

German beer

By law, beer must contain nothing but **hops**, **barley**, and water. This "Purity Law" was passed in 1516, and is still in force today.

Kaffee und Kuchen (Coffee and Cake)

A great tradition in Germany is that of older people meeting friends or family in the middle of the afternoon. They will have a chat over a cup of coffee and a delicious cake. This weekly get-together is a very important part of life in Germany.

Germans meet for coffee or lunch and a chat at a café in Regensburg.

hops climbing plant used in brewing beer

Fresh food

Although there are some giant supermarkets to be found in Germany, most people prefer to buy fresh food daily. Early in the morning, they will go to the local baker's shop to buy fresh bread or rolls for breakfast. Even for lunch or dinner, people will buy and cook food on the same day – meat, fish, vegetables, and fruit. Many towns have a market that is open once or twice a week, and these are popular places for buying fresh fruit and vegetables.

The ice-cream parlour

Young people in Germany enjoy meeting up after school. They will often sit and chat with friends over an exotic ice cream in one of the many small cafés or ice-cream parlours. There are so many different flavours to choose from, it would take a long time to try them all!

Almost every town and village in Germany has its own market. Most people buy their fresh produce here.

WORD BANK immigrants people who move from their own country and settle in another

Favourite dishes

At home, families will usually eat a mixture of traditional German and international dishes. There is also a lot of choice if you want to eat out at a restaurant. Turkish, Spanish, Greek, and Asian restaurants can be found almost everywhere in Germany.

The most common international food available is Italian. The Italians were the first **immigrants** to settle in Germany in large numbers, so it isn't really surprising that you can find so many Italian restaurants!

Cologne is filled with squares lined with restaurants and cafés, where people can eat inside or in the fresh air.

Turkish food

Turks are now the largest immigrant group in Germany. The best-known Turkish food is the "döner"– meat sliced from a rotating spit and put in an enormous bread roll with salad and a hot sauce. Their shops, which specialize in Turkish fruit and vegetables, are very popular in Germany.

City life

Berlin

You are here!

You have enjoyed the sights of Cologne, so you decide to see what some of Germany's other cities are like. The majority of Germans – 87 percent – now live in towns and cities. Since the two parts of Germany were joined again in 1990, the population of the capital, Berlin, has grown dramatically. This seems like a good place to find out what everyday life is like in the cities.

Berlin – the new capital

Your train pulls into Berlin's new main station. Before it was completed, this was the largest building site in Europe. Now it is a crossroads, where international trains running from the north of Europe to the south meet those running from the west to the east.

Families divided

The Berlin Wall divided the city between 1961 and 1989. West Berlin was encircled and became a kind of island in East Germany. During this period, travel between the two parts of the city was virtually impossible. Families and friends were not only separated, but lived in different countries.

Berlin·
EAST GERMANY

WEST GERMANY

Fast fact
While the city of Berlin was divided, more than 160 people were killed attempting to cross from East Berlin to West Berlin.

WORD BANK   urban relating to a city or built-up area

Despite this, your first impression of Germany's capital is not one of noise, traffic, and people hurrying about their business. The main station seems to be at the edge of a huge park. This is Berlin's famous Tiergarten, one of the places where Berliners love to stroll, cycle, skate, or just sit and watch the world go by.

You saw something similar in Munich – its vast "English Garden" right in the heart of the city. Many German people choose to live in apartments in the centre of a city, and these **urban** parks mean that they have wonderful green space on their doorsteps.

▲ Germans enjoy watersports such as sailing and windsurfing at the Wannsee in Berlin.

The Tiergarten in Berlin is a huge green space in the middle of the city. ▼

Berlin's beaches

You might think that the Berliners have a long trip to the seaside, but they don't. The city has its own beaches, mainly at the Wannsee. This is an area with two large lakes, which is just half an hour by train from Berlin. Families flock to enjoy the sun and sand close to their home during the summer months.

The Government district

When the Government moved back to Berlin in 1991, many new buildings had to be constructed. Some of the old buildings, such as the Reichstag (the parliament building), were completely **renovated**. Among the new buildings is the Chancellery, the German equivalent of the White House and 10 Downing Street.

Rebuilding Berlin

Although Berlin has been a **united** city again for more than fifteen years, spending time there makes you realize that the ghosts of the two cities (East and West Berlin) are still visible.

After the destruction caused during World War II, the two parts of the city were rebuilt under two different systems. The centre of the **communist** East Berlin was reshaped to allow huge military parades on its wide avenues and squares, and to house many people in high-rise apartments. West Berlin, on the other hand, was rebuilt in much the same way as it had been before the war.

Many centres

Exploring Berlin you wonder where the city centre actually is. Important landmarks and attractions are found in both parts of the city. Unlike many other capital cities in the world, Berlin is not the place where everything important in Germany happens.

The Chancellery is known locally as the "Federal Washing Machine" because of its colour and shape!

WORD BANK   renovated restored or rebuilt

The biggest German airport, for example, is in Frankfurt am Main, which is also the German financial centre and the headquarters of the European Bank. Hamburg is the media capital of Germany, Munich has the largest university, and Stuttgart a world-famous ballet. Many other cities have museums and galleries with important collections, theatres that are admired all over the world, and major concert venues.

Leisure time

Since Berlin became one city again, it has become one of the most popular centres for young people in Europe. There is a thriving music scene here, and young people enjoy the nightclubs and concerts that are held in Berlin's many venues.

The Sony Centre in the Potsdamer Platz in Berlin was completed in 2000. It contains shops, restaurants, offices, museums, and cinemas.

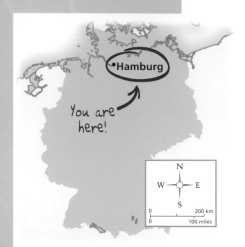

•Hamburg

You are here!

N
W E
S

0   200 km
0   100 miles

Hamburg

Hamburg is Germany's second-largest city (after Berlin). It is a very old city, and people have been living here since the 9th century. They first settled here because of its situation on the River Elbe. The city has been nicknamed the "gateway to the world", because more than five million people travelled through Hamburg from their native countries to look for a better life in other countries in the 19th and early 20th centuries.

Hamburg has 1.7 million inhabitants. Although London has nearly nine million people, Hamburg is more than twice the area. The people here generally have a very high standard of living and the city never seems overcrowded.

Hamburg festivals

Hamburg hosts several festivals throughout the year. One of the most important is the Filmfest Hamburg, which is held in September. There are also street festivals such as the harbour festival, and music festivals, where musicians from all over the world come and play.

The **port** of Hamburg lies on the River Elbe, which flows into the North Sea.

WORD BANK   gable triangular piece of wall between two sloping roofs

A city by the sea

The city is one of the world's greatest seaports. There are many beautiful houses and other buildings here, left over from when Hamburg was a rich **merchant** city. Many of these buildings are made from red brick and have high **gables**. You can only find this style of architecture on the northern coast of Germany.

You make a trip to the famous fish market, which takes place every Sunday morning. It starts at 5 a.m. in the summer, and if you want to enjoy it all and sample some of the local fish specialities, you should be there early. It finishes late in the morning, so that people can go to church. Here in Hamburg, many people go to St Michael's. This is just one of many beautiful old cathedrals that can be found all over Germany.

Germany's cathedrals

The north of Germany is mainly Protestant and the south mainly Catholic. St Michael's, in Hamburg, was built in the Protestant style, but Germany's two greatest cathedrals are both Catholic. These can be found in Cologne and Aachen (the oldest cathedral in Northern Europe).

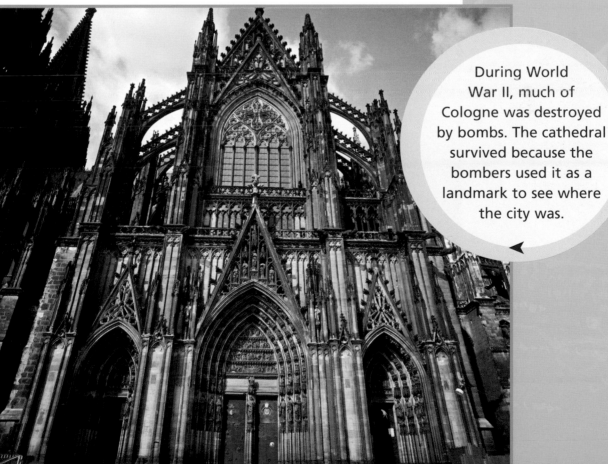

During World War II, much of Cologne was destroyed by bombs. The cathedral survived because the bombers used it as a landmark to see where the city was.

merchant someone who sells goods

Life in the countryside

You are here!

You have experienced life in the cities, but what is life like for those living in Germany's **rural** areas? You decide to spend some time in the flat countryside of Mecklenburg-Vorpommern in the north-east. The landscape here is very different from that in the south. There are plenty of long straight roads, lined with poplar trees, which make it easy to explore this area by bicycle.

Farming

This is a farming region, and there are hundreds of fields and meadows. There is very little industry, and people live in small villages. Many of the young people who once lived here have moved to the cities because there are better job opportunities there.

Village communities

Small German towns and villages pride themselves on their community life. Even a village with fewer than 1,000 people will have clubs catering for all sorts of activities from card-playing and bowling, to choir groups and **allotments**.

Dairy farming is an important industry in Germany. Along with France, it is the largest milk-producing country in the **European Union**.
➤

WORD BANK   allotment small area where people grow fruit, vegetables, and flowers
European Union group of countries that help each other with trade

Fishing

Along the Baltic and North Sea coastlines, there is a thriving fishing industry. Fishermen sometimes go out as far as the Atlantic Ocean to catch fish. Herring, mackerel, and cod are the main fish caught in the waters around Germany.

Tourism

The countryside in this region is unspoilt, the air is clean, and there is lots of wildlife. Because of its natural beauty, this area on the Baltic Sea has become increasingly popular with tourists. Along the coast and on the islands of the Baltic Sea, new hotels and holiday resorts have been built.

Although tourism creates many jobs for local people, it can damage the peacefulness and natural beauty of that area.

Voluntary Fire Service

Germany's smaller towns and villages do not employ full-time firefighters. Instead, they have a great tradition of a voluntary fire brigade. Always ready to leave their paid jobs when an emergency arises, these fire brigades are the centrepiece of village festivals.

rural relating to the countryside

Farming products

The main farming products are milk, pork, cereals, and beef. Farms near cities often specialize in vegetables and fruit, selling them in their own shops or the local market. Some farmers grow **fodder** such as maize and broad beans, and oil plants such as sunflower.

Hi-tech farming

You pay a visit to one of the farms in the region, and are surprised at how hi-tech it is. Even the pigs are not fed by hand any more, but by a computerized feeding system. The increased use of machinery on farms means that farmers do not need to employ as many people as they did in the past. This has resulted in fewer jobs in the countryside, and is one of the reasons why young people are moving to the cities.

The farmer explains that generally, only the larger farms are successful. Some of the smaller farms cannot even make enough money to support a family. The villages, which were once the centres of true farming communities, have become residential areas for people who work in nearby towns and cities. It is cheaper to live in the countryside.

Farmers do not only grow food for **export**. Many of them sell their produce at local markets.

Organic farming

The amount of organic farmland in Germany was three times greater in 2004 than it had been ten years earlier. People are now more aware of the damage caused by chemicals and fertilizers. Less food is produced, and although this means that people have to pay more for it, they are happy to do so if it means well-produced food and well-kept animals.

People cycle through an oil-seed plant field in the German countryside.

An old fortress stands next to a vineyard in the Mosel wine-growing region.

Vineyards

Germany produces a lot of wine. The main wine-producing areas are the Rhine, Mosel, and Main regions. It is fascinating to visit the vineyards and see how the wine is made. More than 1,000 wine festivals and fairs are celebrated in Germany every year.

It's time to head back to Berlin to find out a bit more about the German people, and everyday life in Germany. You are surprised to find so many children and teenagers in the street already at 7.15 a.m. The school day begins at 7.30 or 7.45 a.m., and many young people have to get up at 6 a.m. to get to school in time.

School life

There are three different types of secondary school, depending on a student's abilities. The Gymnasium is the highest level, and this ends with a university entrance examination (Abitur) after eight or nine years.

First day of school

To celebrate a child's first day of school, parents or friends give the child a *Schultüte*. This is a big colourful cardboard cone filled with sweets and school items such as a pencil case and a pen.

Brightly coloured cones filled with sweets and gifts are given to children to celebrate their first day at school.

WORD BANK kindergarten nursery school

Students in secondary school have between 30 and 36 lessons a week, so although they start early, they don't get home early. As many students also enjoy activities outside lesson-time – such as music, drama, or sport either in school or in a club – you wonder how they manage to do it all!

English-speakers

As you chat to the students, you realize that most of them speak English very well. All children start learning English while they are still at primary school, and most of the pop music they listen to is in English, so they speak and understand the language well. Even when they speak German, you notice that they use several English words.

Kindergarten

Before starting school at the age of six, most German children will have spent two or three years in **kindergarten**.

School years

Students can leave full-time school at the age of fifteen, but must attend school part-time until they are eighteen. In general, people leave secondary school at fifteen or sixteen to enter a professional training scheme for three years, or they stay in school until they are eighteen or nineteen and then go to university.

There are usually around 30 students per class in a secondary school.

Ethnic groups

Nine percent of the population of Germany are **ethnic minorities**. A quarter of these are Turkish, and the rest come from many different countries. A lot of **immigrants** have lived in Germany for a very long time, but many of them keep their customs and traditions instead of adopting German ways.

Asylum seekers

After World War II, Germany allowed anyone who suffered political or religious **persecution** in their native country to enter Germany as an **asylum seeker**. Between 1990 and 1993, so many people came to settle in Germany that the law had to be changed to restrict the numbers.

Learning German

Speaking German is very important for immigrants who want to settle in Germany. Since 1990, people applying for German nationality have to pass a German language test. Children of immigrants are now encouraged to go to **kindergarten**, where they can learn German while playing and having fun with other children.

In the early 1990s, so many asylum seekers came to Germany that special centres had to be set up to give them advice and find them places to live.

asylum seeker someone who moves to another country because conditions are bad in their own

Multicultural Germany

The arrival of people from so many different countries has changed the cultural life of Germany, and has made it a very **multicultural** society. Not only can you eat all kinds of different foods, you can also learn to play African drums, do belly dancing, listen to Turkish-German comedians on television, and keep healthy with tai chi and Chinese medicine.

Guest workers

The first immigrants came to Germany during the late 1950s and early 1960s, during a period called the "Economic Miracle". People came mostly from other European countries to work in Germany. At the time, there were not enough people to cope with all the work in Germany, so these immigrants were welcomed.

Chinese forms of exercise such as tai chi are popular in Germany. People gather together to practise in parks like this in Hamburg.

persecution when people are treated badly because of their political or religious beliefs

Dancing

Dancing is a popular pastime in Germany. Students at dance-schools will learn most of the classic dances like the waltz, tango, jive, and the Cha Cha Cha, but disco dancing and salsa are also taught. Teenagers enjoy going to "dance balls" to show off their skills!

People take a walk through the picturesque countryside of Bavaria.

Leisure time

Germans spend their free time in many different ways. On Sundays, many shops are not allowed to open, except bakeries for people to buy their morning rolls. This doesn't mean that city centres are empty, though! Many people stroll around and look at shops, or have a coffee in one of the many cafés. Some of them go to museums or exhibitions, perhaps visit their local park for a picnic, or go swimming. Sunday is also a day for visiting family and friends.

A passion for health

One favourite pastime is the Sunday walk. Woods and parks are full of people walking and enjoying the fresh air. Many people jog or cycle through the forests. Many Germans have a passion for health and fitness, and new ways of exercising body and mind are always being introduced.

Relaxation is popular, too. Visiting a spa has been a popular pastime for a long time. Spending a weekend or a whole week in one of the many new "wellness" hotels is a modern trend, but also a very expensive one. For those who can't afford that, there is always the option to join one of the many sports clubs or gyms to keep fit.

Visit a spa

Many towns in Germany have a name that begins with "Bad". This is German for "bath" or "spa". These places offer special treatments to relieve the stress of working life. There are more than 160 spas across Germany, offering all different types of treatments, including mineral and mud baths.

Germans enjoy the thermal baths at Baden Baden, Germany's most famous spa town.

Everywhere you go, such as shopping centres and train and bus stations, you see not one but several different-coloured litter bins.

Wind power

Germany has Europe's largest wind farm. It also has the largest number of wind farms in the world. It is estimated that by 2010, 12.5 percent of the power used in Germany will be generated by wind. This is a very environmentally friendly way of generating power.

Recycling

Germany is one of the most environmentally aware countries in Europe. The bins are for people to separate their drinks cans from waste paper, ready for recycling. Even houses have more than one bin and waste must be separated.

Glass and plastic bottles, and even cans, now cost more than they once did. The cost includes a deposit to encourage people to take the bottle back to the shop instead of throwing it away. This has led to a big reduction in the amount of waste glass and metal.

Most homes in Germany use special bins that allow people to separate waste into different types so it can be recycled.

Reducing air pollution

The Germans love cars – especially fast cars! Germany is the home of Mercedes, BMW, Porsche, and autobahns without speed limits. However, the Government is aware of the effect that cars have on the environment. Strict controls and higher taxes for old and big, petrol-guzzling cars have encouraged more and more people to drive eco-friendly cars. Germany is also now the home of the eco-friendly Smart car.

Germany's forests are famous worldwide.

The Smart car is very small and can be almost completely recycled.

Saving the forests

Towards the end of the 1970s, it became clear that Germany's forests were dying. Almost one-third of the country is covered in trees, but air pollution was killing the forests. By 1996, only 43 percent were considered healthy. New laws were introduced to force industries and vehicles to reduce air pollution.

In a short time you have been able to travel to many parts of the country, and have seen many fascinating places and met lots of interesting people. There are still so many places to go, though. So, what will it be – stay or go?

Who speaks German?

Germany is the national language of Austria. It is also the language of 65 percent of the population of Switzerland. It is also spoken in Luxembourg, parts of northern Italy, and Belgium.

Still to see and do

Dresden, in Saxony, was once one of the most beautiful cities in Europe, but its centre was almost totally destroyed by bombs during World War II. It is now being restored to its former glory. The rebuilding from ruins of the Church of Our Lady was completed in 2005. You could take a boat trip down the River Elbe to get there.

New Palace – just one of the amazing palaces you can find in Potsdam.

Potsdam, in Brandenburg, is where Frederick the Great, King of Prussia, had his palaces. It is also where the famous conference between the victorious leaders was held at the end of World War II. Potsdam is only half an hour from Berlin by train.

If you are feeling brave, you could head to Brocken, in the Harz Mountains, where witches are said to gather. Or perhaps you could go to Wittenburg, where Martin Luther lived – the founder of the Protestant Christian Church.

German stories

You may think that you have never read anything German, but you probably have. What about Cinderella, Sleeping Beauty, or Little Red Riding Hood? They are all fairy tales from the books of the Brothers Grimm (Jakob and Wilhelm). They published their collection almost 200 years ago.

You could take a ride on an old steam train through the Harz Mountains.

Find out more

World Wide Web

If you want to find out more about Germany, you can search the Internet using keywords such as these:

- Germany
- Berlin
- River Rhine

You can also find your own keywords by using headings or words from this book. Try using a search directory such as www.google.co.uk.

Destination Detectives can find out more about Germany by using the books and websites listed below.

The German Embassy

The German Embassy in your own country has lots of information about Germany. You can find out about the different regions, the best times to visit, special events, including festivals, and all about German culture. The German Embassy in the United Kingdom can be found at: www.german-embassy.org.uk

Further reading

Countries of the World: Germany by Sonja Schanz and Gerry Donaldson (Evans Brothers, 2004)

Nations of the World: Germany by Greg Nickles (Raintree, 2003)

Take Your Camera: Germany by Ted Park (Raintree, 2004)

The Changing Face of Germany by Sonja Schanz (Raintree, 2002)

The Fall of the Berlin Wall by Patricia Levy (Raintree, 2002)

The Rhine by Ronan Foley (Hodder Wayland, 2005)

World Tour: Germany by Christopher Mitten (Raintree, 2004)

Timeline

1455
Johann Gutenberg publishes the first printed book, a Bible, in Mainz, Germany.

1517
Martin Luther protests against the Catholic Church in Wittenburg, starting the Protestant Reformation in Europe.

1835
The first railway opens in Germany.

1871
The German **states** are **united** under Wilhelm of Prussia, creating the German Empire.

1918
Germany is defeated in World War I.

1920s
Economic crisis in Germany. Many people are unemployed.

1933
Adolf Hitler becomes **Chancellor** of Germany at the head of the National Socialist (Nazi) Party.

1936
The Olympic Games are held in Berlin.

1938
Kristallnacht – Jewish synagogues attacked.

1939
Germany invades Poland, and World War II begins.

1945
Germany is defeated in World War II. The country is divided into East Germany and West Germany.

1949
Bonn becomes the capital of West Germany.

1961
Work begins on the Berlin Wall.

1982
Helmut Kohl becomes Chancellor of Germany.

1989
The Berlin Wall is pulled down, reuniting East and West Germany.

1990
Germany is officially reunited as one country.

1991
The capital of the united Germany moves back to Berlin.

1998–2005
Gerhard Schroeder is Chancellor of Germany.

2001
The German Government signs an agreement to phase out nuclear energy.

2002
The Euro becomes Germany's currency.

Germany – facts & figures

The German flag consists of three equal bands of black, red, and gold. The black and red are the colours that were worn by German soldiers during the war against France in the 19th century. The gold was added to create a flag similar to the French flag, which was a symbol of revolution.

People and places

- Population: 82.4 million.
- Life expectancy: men – 76 years; women – 82 years.
- Highest point: Zugspitze (2,962 metres/9,718 feet).

Trade and industry

- Main industries: iron, steel, coal, cement, chemicals.
- Main agricultural products: potatoes, wheat, barley, sugar beets, fruit.
- Workers: 42.6 million.
- Unemployment rate: 11 percent.

Technology

- Mobile phones: 64.8 million.
- Land lines: 54.4 million.
- Internet users: 39 million.
- Internet country code: .de.

Glossary

allotment small area where people grow fruit, vegetables, and flowers

asylum seeker someone who moves to another country because conditions are bad in their own

barge flat-bottomed boat used for transporting goods

barley grain used in making beer

bugle brass instrument like a trumpet but without keys

capitalist society where people can own businesses and resources

chancellor chief minister to a king or emperor

climate typical weather conditions in a region

communist classless society in which resources belong to the community

compensation payment to make up for someone else's loss

Equator imaginary line round the middle of Earth

ethnic group people who share the same customs or nationality

European Union group of countries that help each other with trade

export selling goods to other countries

federal republic group of states under a central government

fodder food for farm animals

gable triangular piece of wall between two sloping roofs

hops climbing plant used in brewing beer

immigrants people who move from their own country and settle in another

inflation rise in how much things cost

kindergarten nursery school

medieval relating to the Middle Ages

merchant someone who sells goods

Middle Ages period of history from around AD 500 to 1500

multicultural made up of people from different cultures or countries

persecution when people are treated badly because of their political or religious beliefs

plains large areas of flat land

port place where ships load or unload cargo

renovated restored or rebuilt

rural relating to the countryside

states areas of Germany that have a level of self-government

tram train that runs on rails through city streets

unite join together

urban relating to a city or built-up area

Index